Writing
Brainstorms

by
Becky Daniel

illustrated by Nancee McClure

Cover by Nancee McClure

Copyright © Good Apple, Inc., 1990

Good Apple, Inc.
1204 Buchanan St., Box 299
Carthage, IL 62321-0299

Table of Contents

GA1172

To the Teacher

Writing Brainstorms is designed to teach early grade students that creative writing is fun! Highly motivating topics have been carefully chosen so that children will enjoy every writing assignment found herein. Topics include shopping lists, cartoons, collages, hidden treasure maps, sky writing, recipes, raps, poems and songs. Children are asked to design menus, want ads and crossword puzzles. Inventions include holidays, sandwiches, new games, playground equipment and new words. Each of the over fifty fun-filled puzzles and activities are guaranteed to make creative writing an enjoyable learning experience for all.

To prepare your students to use the work sheets found herein, it is important to realize that reading the directions may be difficult or impossible for beginning readers. It is therefore suggested that the directions be given in groups and the examples carefully explained before children are sent back to their desks to do independent seatwork.

Bonus activities are found on many pages. These activities are usually more difficult and should not be a requirement. Use the bonus activities for extra credit. Students that complete these should receive special recognition. A class competition could involve keeping track of how many bonus activities are completed by each student and rewarding those that complete a given number. Awards are found on pages 75 and 76 and a special award certificate for bonus activities is included.

GA1172

Scrambled Eggs

Arrange the letters in the words below the boxes to represent the words.

Example: G𐐒SG = scrambled eggs

Name _____

HIGH CHAIR

DOWNTOWN

CIRCLE OF FRIENDS

UNDERSTANDING MOM

SQUARE DANCING

UPTIGHT

Bonus: Make up your own puzzle like those above.

GA1172

Compound Words

Compound words are words made up of two other words. Example: *Footsteps* is a compound word. Look at the pictures and see if you can decide what compound word each pair of pictures represents.

Name _____

Bonus: Choose a compound word and draw two pictures that represent your word.

2

What Did They Say?

What do you think the cartoon characters below are saying to each other? Use the bubbles above their heads to create your own cartoons. Remember, a cartoon is supposed to be funny!

Name _____

Bonus: Draw some characters and use bubbles above their heads to create your own cartoon.

GA1172

Big Ten

Pretend you are going to be taken by helicopter to a deserted island where you must live alone for seven days. The island is warm and has a freshwater pool. You may take only ten different things with you. List each of the ten things and the amount of each you will take. Think before you begin writing. If you forget something important, you may not survive!

Name _____

1. _____

2. _____

3. _____

4. _____

5. _____

6. _____

7. _____

8. _____

9. _____

10. _____

Bonus: If you could take only three of the items you have listed, which would you take? Put a star by them. Could you survive for a week with only those three items?

The Perfect Picnic

Pretend you have been chosen to plan a perfect picnic for you and your friends. Make a list of the things you will need to buy at the market for the perfect picnic.

Name _____

GROCERY LIST ✍

✔ _____
✔ _____
✔ _____
✔ _____
✔ _____
✔ _____
✔ _____
✔ _____
✔ _____
✔ _____
✔ _____
✔ _____
✔ _____
✔ _____

Bonus: Design an invitation announcing your picnic.

GA1172

ABC Suitcase

You are going on a seven-day trip to Disney World. You may take exactly twenty-six items. Each item must begin with a different letter of the alphabet. If you forget something important, you will have to do without it, so plan very carefully!

A _____ N _____

B _____ O _____

C _____ P _____

D _____ Q _____

E _____ R _____

F _____ S __shoes_____

G _____ T _____

H _____ U _____

I _____ V _____

J _____ W _____

K _____ X _____

L _____ Y _____

M __money_____ Z _____

Name _____

Bonus: Again, using the letters of the alphabet, think of twenty-six souvenirs you would like to bring home with you from Disney World.

6

GA1172

Word Factory

Choose a letter blend from column A and a word ending from column B. Put them together to see if they spell a word. Example: bl + ack = black. How many words can you write using combinations from column A and column B? Thirty? Forty?

A

bl
br
cl
cr
dr
fl
fr
gl
gr
pl
thr
sn
str
st
tr
wr

B

ab
ain
ack
ad
am
eam
eep
ane
ame
ing
ook
ow
eet
uff
um
eck

1. _____
2. _____
3. _____
4. _____
5. _____
6. _____
7. _____
8. _____
9. _____
10. _____
11. _____
12. _____
13. _____
14. _____
15. _____
16. _____
17. _____
18. _____
19. _____
20. _____

21. _____
22. _____
23. _____
24. _____
25. _____
26. _____
27. _____
28. _____
29. _____
30. _____
31. _____
32. _____
33. _____
34. _____
35. _____
36. _____
37. _____
38. _____
39. _____
40. _____

Name _____

Bonus: Can you write ten more words by combining the blends and word endings?

GA1172

The Suggestion Box

If there were a suggestion box in your house, what three suggestions would you give for making your house into a more wonderful place to live? Use the slips below to record your suggestions to Mother, Father or a sibling (brother or sister).

Name _____

To: _____

From: _____

Suggestion: _____

_____

Dear _____,

Suggestion: _____

_____

_____

SUGGESTION

FOR: _____

_____

_____

_____

FROM: _____

_____

Bonus: Write three suggestions to make your classroom a more enjoyable place to learn.

GA1172

Me!

Use pictures and words cut from magazines and newspapers to make a collage that describes the true you. Choose the words and pictures carefully. You want your collage to be accurate.

Name _____

9

Secret Message

Using only letters and words cut from old magazines, write a secret message to a friend. You should decide what message you will spell before you begin cutting and pasting letters.

Name _____

Bonus: Write a sentence of ten or more words using only letters cut from magazines.

10

New Jackets

There is an old adage that says, "Never judge a book by its cover," but still, people often do. Choose your favorite book and design a new cover for it.

Name _____

Bonus: Design a cover for your autobiography.

GA1172

Word Pictures

Using only the letters of words, can you create pictures of the words? See the examples below. Here are some words that you might want to illustrate: dog, net, pencil, cow, car, train, box, man, woman, girl, butterfly, apple, ink, book, worm, fire, lightning, snow, tears, hand, foot, pizza, hot dog, hamburger, sandwich, cookie, ice-cream cone. Choose four and illustrate one in each box below.

Name _____

12

GA1172

Colorful Words

If you color the words below the correct colors, they will take on a whole new meaning. Example: If I color the letter **V** gray, it means gravy (gray V). Think carefully before you color each letter or word below.

Name _____

TV J

N J

N

BOARD

HOUSE

BERRY

BIRD

E

Bonus: Make up a colorful word puzzle of your own.

GA1172

Hidden Treasure

Use the outline of an island below to design the perfect hiding place for treasure. Put mountains, forests, streams, caves, anything you choose on your island. Mark the best hiding place for treasure with a red *X*.   Name _____

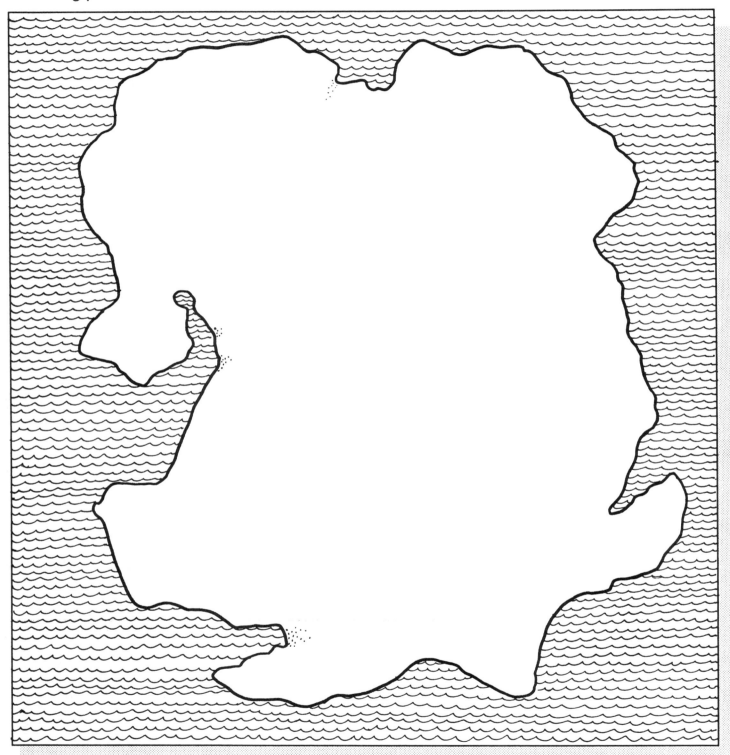

Bonus: Write directions for finding the treasure.

14

Skywriting

Everyone has done something brave, heroic or special that has gone unnoticed by others. What wonderful thing would you like others to know about you? If a skywriter were to write your message high above the clouds, what would it say? Don't be an unsung hero—use the space below to write your message!

Name _____

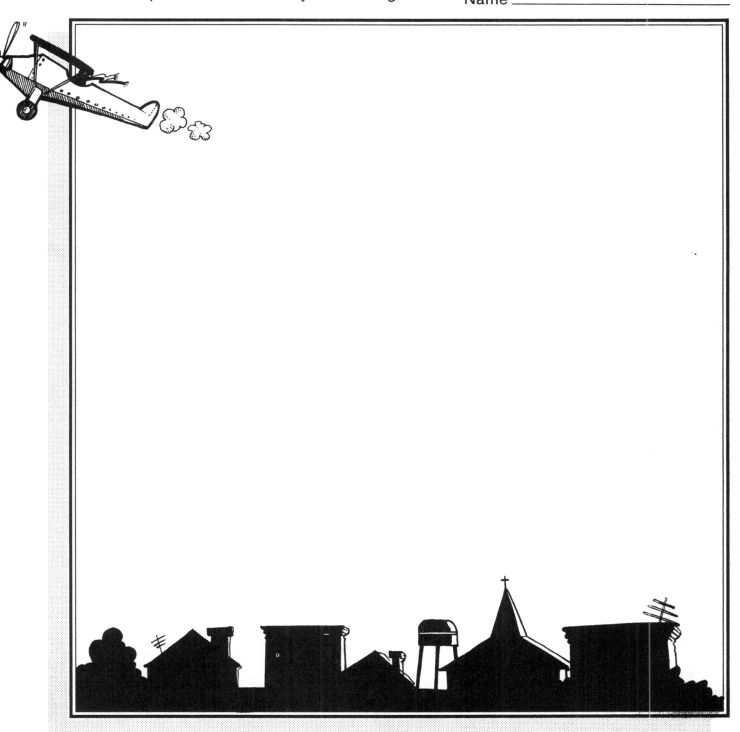

Bonus: What message would you like to tell the world about Mom, Dad or a brother or sister? Write it here.

15

Opening Soon

Pretend there is a new restaurant opening soon in your city. The restaurant is to be the first ever For Kids Only restaurant. You have been chosen to select what foods will appear on the menu. Use the space below to list the choices, a brief description of each and the price, of course!

Name _____

❧ Menu ❧

_____

_____ .... $

_____ .... $

_____ .... $

.... $

Bonus: Think of a good name for a restaurant for kids.

GA1172

Picture Story

Write a story using as many pictures for words as you can. The more pictures and the less words the better!

Name _____

Bonus: Give your picture story to a friend and see if he/she can read it.

17

Me for President

Pretend you have been nominated for President of the United States. Think carefully about the image you want to create. Write a slogan for yourself on the banner. Then list the four things you will stress in your campaign for President on the signs below.

Name _____

Bonus: Design a campaign button for you. Color it. Wear it.

Perfect Friend

Pretend you have been looking for the perfect friend but have not had any luck. You decide to write a want ad to find your perfect friend. Write your ad which should include the qualifications for being the perfect friend in the ad space below.

Name _____

★★★★★ WANT ADS ★★★★★

NEEDED – Best Friend

Must have:

Bonus: Write a want ad for the perfect mother, father or sibling.

GA1172

Young or Old?

Most young people think it would be better to be older. Most older folks think it would be better to go back in time to when they were younger. There are benefits to being young and old. List ten benefits of being a child and ten benefits of being a senior citizen in the spaces provided below.

Name _____

Young

1. _____
2. _____
3. _____
4. _____
5. _____
6. _____
7. _____
8. _____
9. _____
10. _____

Old

1. _____
2. _____
3. _____
4. _____
5. _____
6. _____
7. _____
8. _____
9. _____
10. _____

Bonus: List ten benefits for being middle-aged.

GA1172

Outer Space Satellite

Pretend that you have been invited to create a collage of magazine pictures that show what life on Earth is like. Your collage will be put in a satellite and sent to another galaxy. Choose your pictures carefully so that you give an accurate picture of earthlings.

Name _____

Bonus: What one-word message would you send into outer space?

21

How Far Can You Go?

How far can you go in the maze? You must obtain a signature for each space on the maze. Example: If your best friend wears glasses, he can sign the first space for you. Rules:

1. You may not have a person sign more than one space.

Name _____

2. You must obtain signatures in the order of the spaces in the maze.

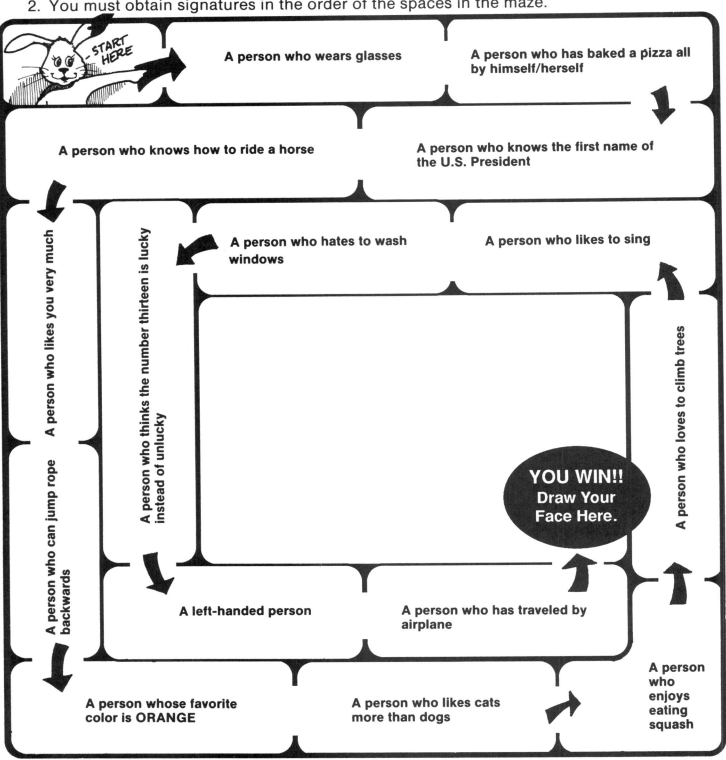

START HERE

A person who wears glasses

A person who has baked a pizza all by himself/herself

A person who knows how to ride a horse

A person who knows the first name of the U.S. President

A person who likes you very much

A person who thinks the number thirteen is lucky instead of unlucky

A person who hates to wash windows

A person who likes to sing

A person who loves to climb trees

A person who can jump rope backwards

YOU WIN!! Draw Your Face Here.

A left-handed person

A person who has traveled by airplane

A person whose favorite color is ORANGE

A person who likes cats more than dogs

A person who enjoys eating squash

Bonus: Color each space in the maze that accurately describes you BLUE.

GA1172

How to Do It!

Write the step-by-step directions for one of the following: tying your shoes, making an ice-cream sundae, building a snowman, decorating a Christmas tree or carving a jack-o'-lantern.

Name _____

1. _____
   _____
2. _____
   _____
3. _____
   _____
4. _____
   _____
5. _____
   _____
6. _____
   _____
7. _____
   _____
8. _____
   _____
9. _____
   _____

Bonus: Write the step-by-step directions for doing something. Give your directions to a friend and see if he/she can guess what your directions are for.

23

GA1172

Typewriter

Using the letters in the word *typewriter*, write as many words as you can. Letters may be used only once unless they appear in the word more than one time. Example: The letter *T* can be used two times in a word because it appears in the word *typewriter* two times. Can you think of twenty?

Name _____

1. _____	11. _____
2. _____	12. _____
3. _____	13. _____
4. _____	14. _____
5. _____	15. _____
6. _____	16. _____
7. _____	17. _____
8. _____	18. _____
9. _____	19. _____
10. _____	20. _____

Bonus: Can you think of twenty more?

GA1172

A New Flavor

I scream, you scream, we all scream for ice cream. But do you ever get bored with the same old flavors? Have you ever dreamed of a uniquely different ice-cream flavor? Think of a flavor that has never been used for ice cream before. Name your new flavor and write the recipe for creating your new ice cream, too.

Name _____

TITLE: _____

RECIPE: _____

Bonus: It is your job to invent a vegetable-flavored ice cream and sell the idea to children. What vegetable will you choose? Write an ad to sell your new veggie ice cream.

25

GA1172

You Choose

Choose three categories of words. Example: three-letter words, sounds, words that begin with the letter Z, girls' names, holidays, colors, etc. Write your three categories at the top of a list below. Then see if you can list ten words that fit each category.

Name _____

1. _____
2. _____
3. _____
4. _____
5. _____
6. _____
7. _____
8. _____
9. _____
10. _____

1. _____
2. _____
3. _____
4. _____
5. _____
6. _____
7. _____
8. _____
9. _____
10. _____

1. _____
2. _____
3. _____
4. _____
5. _____
6. _____
7. _____
8. _____
9. _____
10. _____

Bonus: Think of another word category and list twenty-five words that fit it.

Copyright © 1990, Good Apple, Inc.

26

GA1172

Toothpaste Rapper

A rap is slang for a chant or jingle performed with a definite beat. Sometimes raps rhyme but not always. Write a rap that will sell a new brand of toothpaste. Don't forget to think of a snappy name for your new invention!

Name _____

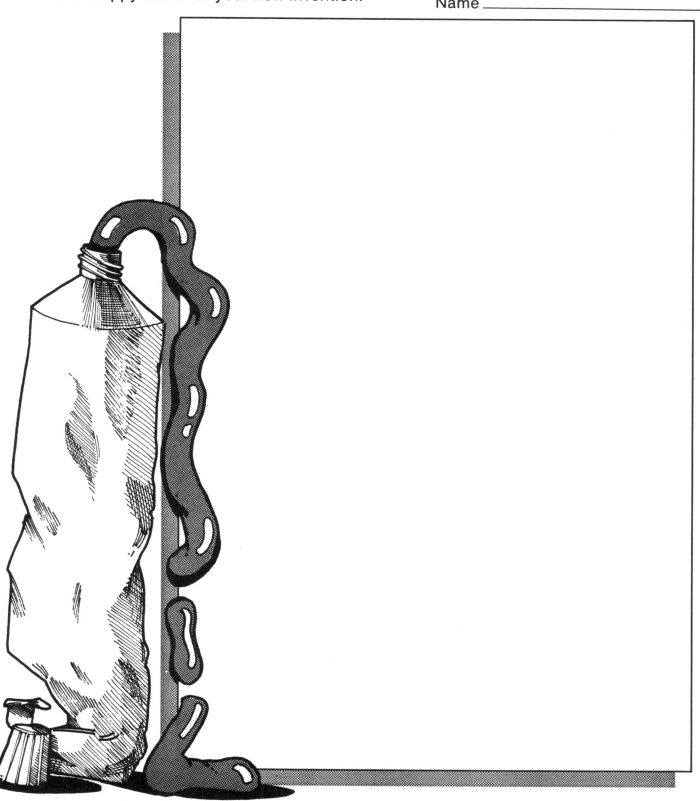

Bonus: Design a wrapper for your new toothpaste.

GA1172

A New Sandwich

Create a new sandwich. Sandwich possibilities are almost endless! The plenteous combinations of meats, cheeses and vegetables that you can cram onto rolls or pack between slices of bread make sandwiches one of the most delicious dishes available. Your new sandwich should be original and healthy. Include the name of your new creation, a list of ingredients and directions for building your sandwich.

Name _____

TITLE: _____

RECIPE: _____

_____

_____

_____

_____

_____

GA1172

Invent a New Holiday

Holidays are filled with traditions that make the day special. What are your favorite holiday traditions? What new traditions would you like to see happen on holidays? Invent a new holiday. Give it a name and date to be celebrated. Then explain how your new holiday is to be celebrated. List the foods, decorations and activities that will make your new holiday a big success.

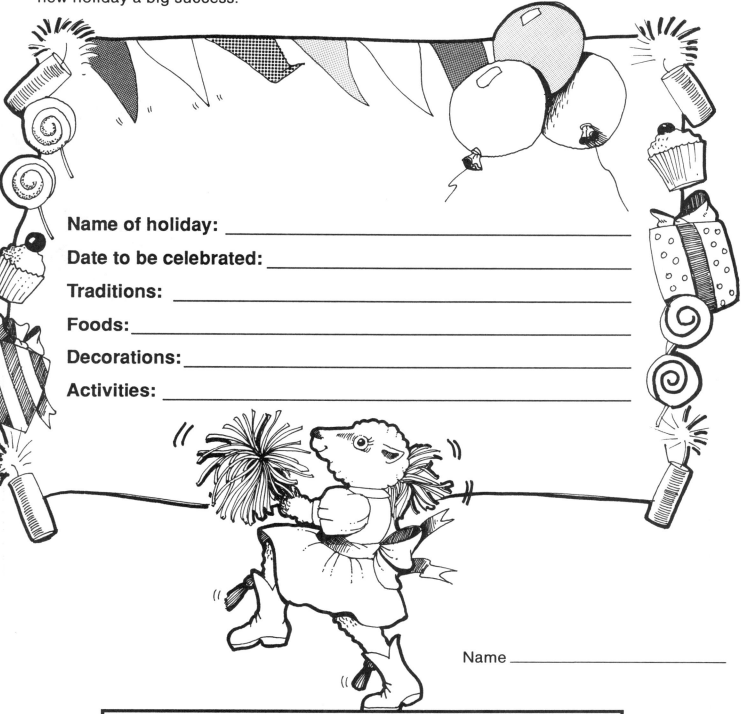

Name of holiday: _____

Date to be celebrated: _____

Traditions: _____

Foods: _____

Decorations: _____

Activities: _____

Name _____

Bonus: Draw a logo for your new holiday that will help others want to celebrate it, too. Example: A jack-o'-lantern is a symbol for Halloween.

GA1172

Invent a New Game

Invent a new game! Name the game and list the equipment needed to play. Give step-by-step directions and rules for your new game. In the box at the bottom of the page, please include a diagram of the board or playing field if appropriate.

Name _____

Name of the game: _____

Equipment needed: _____

Directions for playing: _____

_____

_____

Rules: _____

_____

_____

_____

GA1172

Don't Bug Me!

Below are illustrations for folding an origami bug. Your job is to write the directions for creating the pesky little critter.

Name _____

1.

2.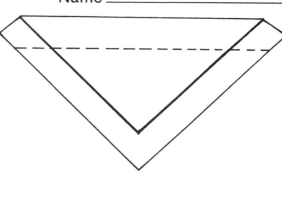

_____
_____
_____

_____
_____
_____
_____
_____

3.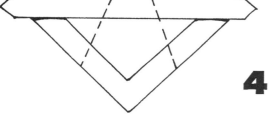

4.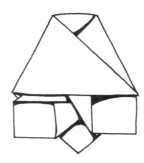

5.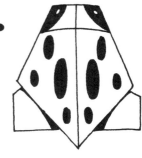

_____
_____
_____
_____
_____
_____
_____
_____

_____
_____
_____
_____
_____
_____
_____

_____
_____
_____
_____
_____
_____

Bonus: Write directions for folding a paper airplane.

GA1172

Just the Facts, Please

Describe one room in your house. Include every detail, colors, size, shape, what the room is used for, etc. Draw every item of furniture in the room. Don't leave out any details!

_____

_____

_____

_____

_____

_____

_____

_____

_____

Name _____

Bonus: Draw a picture of your dream bedroom. Then write a paragraph describing it.

Irony

Irony is a humorous expression in which the real meaning is the opposite of what is said. Underline the ironic word(s) in each sentence below. Then write on the line that follows each sentence the real meaning of the underlined word. The first one has been completed for you.

1. <u>Very clever.</u> Now you broke it.

   Not very clever

2. That was graceful. You tripped over your own feet.

   _____

3. I would simply love to do more homework.

   _____

4. I cannot wait to eat my spinach.

   _____

5. Don't rush. I can wait here all day.

   _____

Name _____

Bonus: Write an ironic sentence.

GA1172

Four Seasons

Pretend you have been chosen to design a poster that shows the weather for all four seasons. Use the circular poster below to illustrate what each season is like in the area in which you live. Then use the outside circle to write one sentence that describes each season.

Name _____

Bonus: Research to find out what the first day of each season will be this year. When is the first day of winter? When is the first day of spring? When is the first day of autumn? When is the first day of summer?

34

Outer Space Bars

Some candy bars have outer space names. Example: Milky Way and Mars. Choose an outer space name for a new candy bar. Put the name of the bar and a design for the wrapper on the candy bar wrapper below. List the ingredients, too.

Ingredients: _____

Name _____

Bonus: Write an ad that would help sell your candy bar.

GA1172

Noun or Verb?

A noun is a person, place or thing. A verb is an action. Example: The man walked. man = noun, walked = verb. Some words can be nouns or verbs, depending on how they are used in a sentence. If a noun is used as a verb, you can invent some really silly riddles. Example: Have you ever seen a jelly roll? Jelly roll is a noun, but if you read the roll as a verb, the sentence has a whole new meaning. Pretend that some of the nouns in the sentences below are verbs. Draw a picture to illustrate the new meaning of each sentence.

Name _____

Have you ever seen an egg roll?

Have you ever seen a lamb chop?

Have you ever seen a paper box?

Have you ever seen a toy box?

Bonus: Write a riddle like those above.

36

GA1172

A, My Name Is Amy

Print or write your first name in cursive on the dotted line. Fold the paper on the dotted line and trace your name on the underside of the fold.
Example:

Then use different colored crayons to trace around the letters until the whole space is filled.

Name _____

- -

Bonus: Do this for your last name, too.

GA1172

A Dozen Things to Do with Popcorn

Make a list of twelve things to use popped popcorn for besides eating it as a snack.
Example: Use popped corn for packing when mailing fragile things through the mail.

Name _____

1. _____
2. _____
3. _____
4. _____
5. _____
6. _____
7. _____
8. _____
9. _____
10. _____
11. _____
12. _____

Bonus: List twelve things to use marbles for besides playing with them.

GA1172

Make Them Rhyme

Poems don't have to rhyme. But just for fun, choose rhyming words to complete each pair of sentences below.

Name _____

My name is _____ ,

I'm happy to _____ .

I love to _____ ,

When the day is _____ .

Walking in the _____ ,

On a star-filled _____ .

When I think, I think of _____ ,

When I dream, I dream of _____ .

Write a short rhyming poem in the heart.

Bonus: Write a six-line rhyming poem.

GA1172

Going Home Again

Draw a map and give step-by-step directions for getting from your house to your school.

Name _____

Map

Directions: _____

_____

_____

_____

_____

_____

_____

_____

_____

_____

Bonus: Draw a map and give step-by-step directions to get from your house to your best friend's house.

GA1172

Invent New Words

New words often emerge in our changing world. Before computers, a DISC was something found in your back. A PROGRAM was something you watched on TV, and PRINT was what you did before you learned to write in cursive. Make up some new words of your own. Give each word's definition.

Name _____

1. _____ _____

2. _____ _____

3. _____ _____

4. _____ _____

5. _____ _____

6. _____ _____

7. _____ _____

8. _____ _____

Bonus: Using the symbols in the dictionary, write the correct pronunciation for each of your new words.

GA1172

New Playground Equipment

Have you ever dreamed of new playground equipment? Do you ever wish your school had a completely new and unique piece of equipment on your playground? If you could have the equipment of your dreams built for your school, what would it look like? Draw a picture of it. Then explain how it is to be used.

Name _____

_____

_____

_____

_____

_____

_____

Bonus: Think of a name for your new playground equipment.

GA1172

Making Lists

Make a list of everything you would need to do each thing shown in the boxes below. Think hard. Don't forget one single thing!

Name _____

pop popcorn

✗ _____
✗ _____
✗ _____
✗ _____
✗ _____
✗ _____
✗ _____
✗ _____
✗ _____
✗ _____

make homemade ice cream

✗ _____
✗ _____
✗ _____
✗ _____
✗ _____
✗ _____
✗ _____
✗ _____
✗ _____
✗ _____

plant a garden

✗ _____
✗ _____
✗ _____
✗ _____
✗ _____
✗ _____
✗ _____
✗ _____
✗ _____
✗ _____

build a bicycle

✗ _____
✗ _____
✗ _____
✗ _____
✗ _____
✗ _____
✗ _____
✗ _____
✗ _____
✗ _____

Bonus: Make a list of everything you would need to build a fence.

GA1172

Study the Ants

Have you seen any ants working lately? Go outside and watch ants for awhile. Then describe what you saw or write a fictional story about an ant family.

Name _____

Celebrate Yourself

Celebrate yourself by writing an acrostic poem about YOU. The letters of your first name are the first letters of the words in your poem. Each word in the poem should tell something about you. Example:

Name _____

B rave

E nergetic

C razy

K ite flyer

Y oga

Bonus: Use the letters of your last name to write another acrostic poem about yourself.

GA1172

Lettering Fun

Using only the letters of words, can you give the definitions of the words by the way they are written? Example:

Here are some words you might want to try: tall, short, skinny, wiggly, straight, spooky, bumpy, smooth, squeezed, squished, fancy, brilliant, dreamy, sparkling, shining.

Bonus: Write your name in a fashion that describes you.

46

GA1172

My Crossword Puzzle

Everyone has worked at least one crossword puzzle, but have you ever written one? Here is your chance. Begin by choosing a word for each space in the puzzle. Record the answers on another sheet of paper. Remember the first letter of across and down words with the same number will always be the same. Below write the clues for your puzzle.

Name _____

ACROSS:

1. _____

3. _____

5. _____

DOWN:

1. _____

2. _____

4. _____

Bonus: Give your crossword puzzle to a friend and see if he can solve it.

47

Brush, Brush, Brush Your Teeth

Using the tune of the song "Row, Row, Row Your Boat," make up your own original song to encourage people to brush their teeth. The first line of the four-line song has been written for you.

Name _____

Brush, brush, brush your teeth

_____

_____

_____

_____

_____

Bonus: Using the tune of the song "Twinkle, Twinkle, Little Star," write a song to teach children how to count to twenty.

GA1172

Lost in the Woods

Name _____

Use the campground map below to finish the Lost in the Woods story. Write a tale of your adventure. Describe the things that you see and the directions you are going. Make your path and story as long as possible. How should it end? You must decide!

One day as I went walking in the woods I discovered that I couldn't find my way back to my tent. I walked and walked

LUMBER MILL

RANGER STATION

49

GA1172

Read It on Their Faces

You can tell a lot about what a person is thinking by the expression on his face. Look carefully at each face below and decide what each one is thinking. Fill in the bubble over each head with the words that you think he/she is thinking.

Name _____

Bonus: Draw three faces and write a caption of thought to match the facial expression for each one.

GA1172

Recipes for Life

Use the recipe cards below to write recipes for a good life. The recipe for a perfect party might be 36 friends, 6 hours to play, 100 pizzas, 30 sodas, 10 chocolate cakes, 6 gallons of vanilla ice cream.

Name _____

Perfect Teacher

Perfect Friend

Perfect Vacation

Bonus: Write the recipe for the perfect pet.

51

How Are They Alike?

List two ways in which the word pairs below are alike. The first one has been completed for you.

1. **popcorn and coconut flakes**
   Both are food and both are white.

2. **bikes and beach balls**

3. **dolphins and dinosaurs**

4. **purple and orange**

5. **hair and apples**

6. **baseball and balloons**

7. **children and mice**

8. **spaghetti and soup**

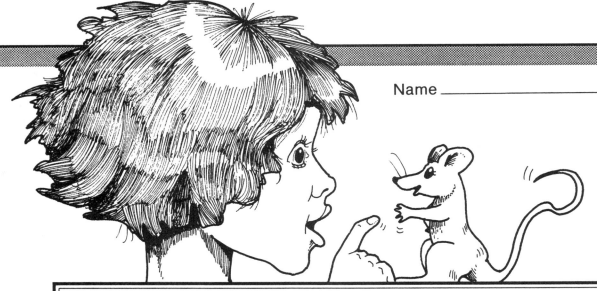

Name _____

Bonus: Make a list of three ways that an antique is like an elephant.

GA1172

A Big Problem

Everyone has something in his life that he considers a big problem. Think carefully and decide what the biggest problem in your life is. Then write it in the box. Think of five solutions to help you solve your problem.

MY
BIG
PROBLEM!

_____

_____

Solution #1 _____

_____

Solution #2 _____

_____

Solution #3 _____

_____

Solution #4 _____

_____

Solution #5 _____

_____

Name _____

Bonus: Decide which of your solutions would be the best. Put a star by it. Try it!

GA1172

Paint Your Van

Pretend you own your own business. You have purchased a van for pickups and deliveries. What would your van look like? What kind of business are you in? What is the name of your business? Color your van to advertise your business.

Name _____

Bonus: Cut a 2" × 5" piece of paper. Use it to design your business card.

GA1172

Advertising Expert

You own an advertising company. It is your job to come up with titles for new products. Below is a list of brand-new things ready for the market—except for a name. Think of a clever title for each product.

1. **Toothpaste that tastes like bubble gum:**

   _____

2. **Cereal with dehydrated strawberries that get fat and juicy when milk is added:**

   _____

3. **A baseball that leaves planet Earth when batted:**

   _____

4. **A rain hat that automatically opens into an umbrella when it gets wet:**

   _____

5. **Bags of popcorn that pop when you place them in sunshine:**

   _____

6. **A machine that reads and completes any homework paper:**

   _____

7. **A headset that makes it possible to hear the thoughts of anyone you are looking at:**

   _____

8. **A bicycle that flies if you pedal fast enough:**

   _____

Name _____

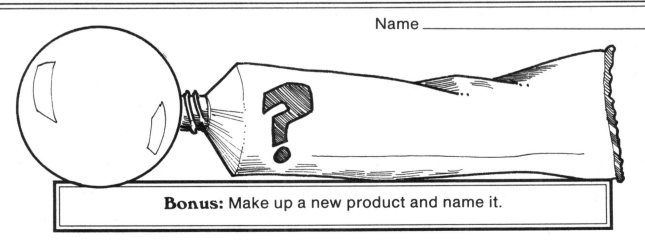

Bonus: Make up a new product and name it.

GA1172

Imagine That!

Answer each "imagine" question below with three complete sentences.

1. **Imagine what it would be like if money grew on trees.**

   a. _____

   b. _____

   c. _____

2. **Imagine what it would be like if you could fly, but no one else could.**

   a. _____

   b. _____

   c. _____

3. **Imagine what it would be like if you awakened one morning to discover that you had grown so much that your legs were hanging off the bed. You stood up and found that you had to bend over to get through your bedroom door.**

   a. _____

   b. _____

   c. _____

4. **You suddenly realized that you could accurately predict the future.**

   a. _____

   b. _____

   c. _____

5. **You went to school one day and discovered that the substitute teacher was your mother.**

   a. _____

   b. _____

   c. _____

Bonus: Choose any one of the five topics above and write a whole story about it.

56

GA1172

The Big Mystery

Pretend that your very best friend has disappeared. The police ask you for help in solving the mystery. In your friend's room you discover that there is a roll of film in his/her camera. When you develop the film, the last four pictures explain what happened to your friend. Draw the photographs that explain where your friend can be found.

1.

2.

3.

4.

Name _____

Bonus: Write a story that tells all about the mysterious disappearance of your best friend.

GA1172

Tongue Twisters

Alliteration is the use of words that begin with the same letter or sound. Tongue twisters use alliteration. Example: Peter picked a peck of pickled peppers. Write a tongue twister using the first sound of your first or last name.

Name _____

Bonus: Write a tongue twister using the first letter of the name of your best friend.

58

Class President

Duck, Lamb and Bear are all running for class president. Design a campaign poster, including a clever slogan for each candidate. Using crayons or markers, color each poster with vivid colors.

Name _____

Bonus: Write a fifty to seventy-five-word campaign speech for your favorite candidate.

GA1172

Twenty Years from Now

Do you ever dream about your future? What do you think your life will be like in twenty years? How old will you be? What profession will you have chosen for yourself? Use the daily schedule below to record what you think you will be doing on a typical weekday twenty years from now.

Name _____

Twenty Years from Now

7:00 _____
_____
8:00 _____
_____
9:00 _____
_____
10:00 _____
_____
11:00 _____
_____
12:00 noon _____
_____
1:00 _____
_____
2:00 _____
_____
3:00 _____
_____

Daily Schedule

4:00 _____
_____
5:00 _____
_____
6:00 _____
_____
7:00 _____
_____
8:00 _____
_____
9:00 _____
_____
10:00 _____
_____
11:00 _____
_____
12:00 _____
_____

Bonus: Repeat this activity, but give a schedule of events for a typical week twenty years from now.

GA1172

What's Inside?

Look at the bag below. Then make a list of twenty possible things that might be inside. Next make a list of twenty things that are definitely not inside the bag.

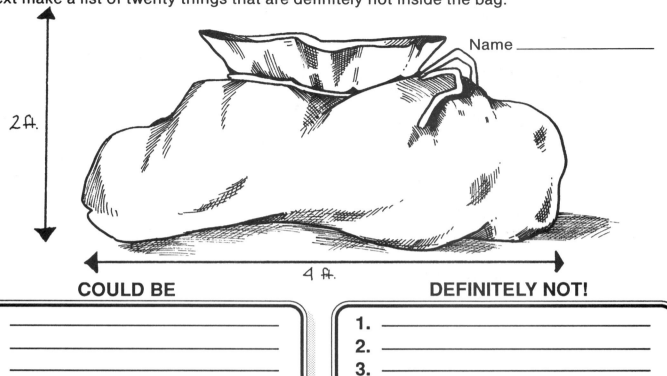

2 ft.

4 ft.

Name _____

COULD BE	DEFINITELY NOT!
1. _____	1. _____
2. _____	2. _____
3. _____	3. _____
4. _____	4. _____
5. _____	5. _____
6. _____	6. _____
7. _____	7. _____
8. _____	8. _____
9. _____	9. _____
10. _____	10. _____
11. _____	11. _____
12. _____	12. _____
13. _____	13. _____
14. _____	14. _____
15. _____	15. _____
16. _____	16. _____
17. _____	17. _____
18. _____	18. _____
19. _____	19. _____
20. _____	20. _____

Bonus: Choose your favorite thing on your list of possibilities and draw it on the bag.

GA1172

Halloween Haunted House

Pretend that you have been chosen to design the school's haunted house for a Halloween carnival. Describe the scary things that you will include in your haunted house.

Name _____

Bonus: Write a fifty-word story about two children that accidentally wander into your haunted house and are really frightened!

GA1172

Duck's Worst Nightmare

Duck has just had his worst nightmare! Describe in detail what Duck's nightmare was about.

Name _____

Bonus: In pictures or words, describe your worst nightmare.

GA1172

The Perfect Classroom

Pretend that you have been chosen to design a classroom that will be a model for all new schools in the United States. The classroom design must be functional, educational and also exciting and relaxing at the same time. In pictures and words, describe in detail the classroom of your dreams.

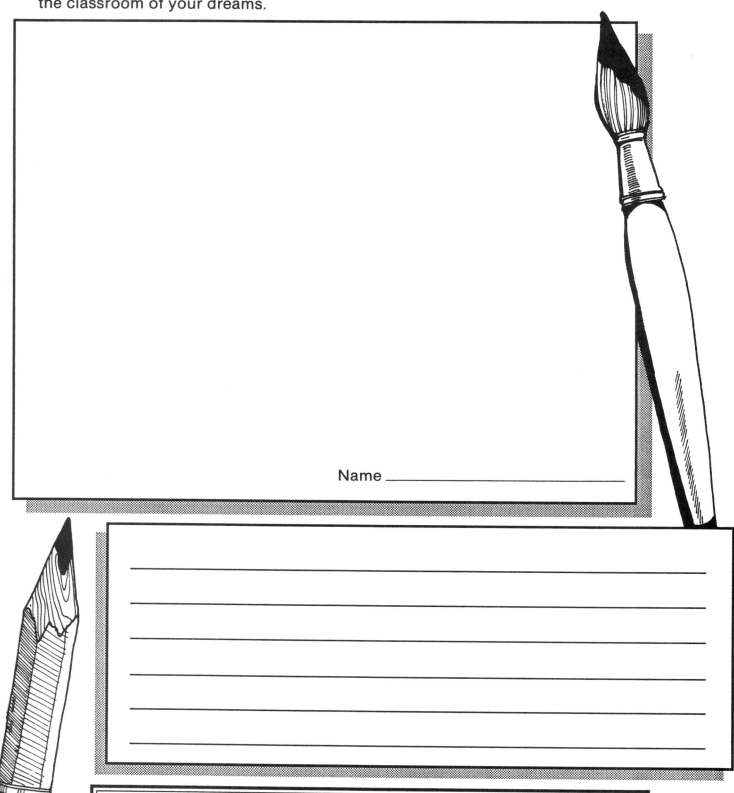

Name _____

_____
_____
_____
_____
_____
_____

Bonus: Draw the outside of the school building that contains the classroom you have just designed.

64

GA1172

Home Schools

Pretend that all children study via computer in their homes instead of going to school to learn. List ten advantages of learning in your own home.

Name _____

Bonus: List ten disadvantages of learning on computers in your home instead of going to school.

65 GA1172

Finish the Day!

When Duck got on the bus to go to school, he discovered that he was wearing his house slippers instead of his shoes. Describe in detail the rest of Duck's school day.

Name _____

Dear Diary,

Bonus: Write a story about the day that Bear accidentally wore his pajamas to school.

66

GA1172

Gold Nuggets!

Pretend that you have invented a machine that turns common stones into real gold nuggets. Explain step-by-step how your machine works.

1. _____

2. _____

3. _____

4. _____

5. _____

6. _____

Name _____

Bonus: Draw a picture of your gold nugget machine.

GA1172

Big, Bad Bully

Every day on the way to school, a big, bad bully stops Lamb and steals her sack lunch. She's afraid to tell anyone, because the bully has threatened to kick her if she tells. List ten things that Lamb can do to help her situation. Be creative and clever. Example: She can bring a terrible tasting sandwich so that the bully won't want to eat her lunch again.

1. _____
2. _____
3. _____
4. _____
5. _____
6. _____
7. _____
8. _____
9. _____
10. _____

Name _____

Bonus: Pick your favorite suggestion above and write a story about what happens when Lamb follows the suggestion.

Help Lamb Decide

Halfway home from school, Lamb remembered that her mother had told her that if she left her umbrella at school one more day, she would be grounded for an afternoon. Lamb looked at her watch and knew that if she went back to school to get the umbrella, she would get home too late to watch her favorite TV program. She knows her mother won't be home until after her favorite program is over. Should she go back and get her umbrella and miss her favorite program or continue home quickly so she can watch the program and let her mother ground her afterwards? You decide. Write a fifty-word story that tells what happens when Lamb does what you think is best.

Name _____

Bonus: Pretend that Lamb did the opposite of what you think she should have done. Write a story telling what happened.

Bear's Unbearable Problem

Today Bear has picked up his new glasses. He doesn't want to wear them to school tomorrow because he thinks that his friends will make fun of him. He's anxious because tomorrow is the first day of second grade for Bear. Pretend that you are one of Bear's friends, and he telephones you asking your advice. What will you tell Bear to help him feel more comfortable beginning a new school year wearing his new glasses?

Name _____

Bonus: Design a button with a slogan, riddle or rhyme that celebrates wearing glasses.

GA1172

Lamb's Lost Watch

Lamb lost her new watch. She has looked for it for over a week. She's afraid to tell Mother Lamb because when her mother gave her the watch, she explained that it was very expensive. The watch was more than just a watch; it was Mother Lamb's way of saying that she thought Lamb was getting grown-up. Lamb decided to write her mother a letter to explain how she felt because in a letter she could organize her thoughts, say everything without being interrupted and express exactly how she felt. Write Lamb's letter.

Name _____

From the Desk of... Lambie Pie

Bonus: Write a letter of response from Mother Lamb.

GA1172

Rabbit's Sweater

Rabbit's grandmother knitted him a new sweater. It was the ugliest sweater that Rabbit had ever seen. He just couldn't wear it to school or even out to play! Rabbit didn't want all of his grandmother's hard work to be wasted, so he wrote a list of reasons why he had to return the sweater and suggested that she give it to his cousin Ralph Rabbit. Rabbit knew that Ralph would like the sweater; it was all his favorite colors. List ten good reasons (that won't hurt Grandma Rabbit's feelings) for returning the sweater.

1. _____
2. _____
3. _____
4. _____
5. _____
6. _____
7. _____
8. _____
9. _____
10. _____

Name _____

Bonus: Put a star by the three most important reasons for returning the sweater.

GA1172

Tiger's Decision

When Tiger came home from school, he smelled smoke. After questioning his big brother, he discovered that he had been smoking Father Tiger's pipe. Brother Tiger told Tiger that if he tells, he will be nothing but a *snitch*. Tiger is torn between telling his parents so they can help Brother Tiger before he develops a bad health habit and not telling because he doesn't want to be a *snitch*. If he tells, he knows that his brother will be in big trouble. If he doesn't tell, his brother may be in even bigger trouble. Write Tiger's thoughts regarding his dilemma.

_____

_____

_____

_____

_____

_____

_____

_____

_____

_____

_____

_____

_____

_____

Name _____

Bonus: Write a story about what happens after Tiger makes his decision to tell or not to tell.

73

Answer Key

Word Factory Page 7

Answers will vary.
Some may include black, blame, bluff, brad, brain, bring, brook, brow, clack, clad, clam, crab, crack, cram, cream, creep, crook, crow, drab, drain, dream, drum, fling, flow, fluff, frame, glad, gleam, glow, glum, grab, grain, grow, greet, gruff, plow, plum, plane, throw, snack, snook, snow, stream, string, street, strum, stab, stain, stack, stream, steep, sting, stuff, train, track, tram, wring, wreck.

Colorful Words Page 13

black and white TV
white or green house
blue or black bird
blue or black berry
red E (ready)
black N (blacken)
blue jay
black board

Typewriter Page 24

Answers may vary.
Some may include write, type, it, pet, tip, pit, wet, yet, were, pew, peer, tie, pie, tree, tire, wire, we, wee, writer, wit.

Don't Bug Me! Page 31

1. Make sure your paper is square. Fold diagonally a little off center as shown.
2. Fold forward as shown.
3. Fold back to form body and legs and overlap underneath.
4. The underside of bug will look like this.
5. The top of bug will look like this. Add eyes.

How Are They Alike? Page 52

Answers will vary.
Possible answers may include:
2. Both are toys and come in bright colors.
3. Both begin with the letter *D* and are animals.
4. Both are colors and have six letters.
5. Both can be red or yellow and are washed.
6. Both are round and have eight letters.
7. Cats like both and they sneak around in the kitchen looking for food.
8. Both begin with the letter *S* and are best eaten while they are still hot.

GA1172

75

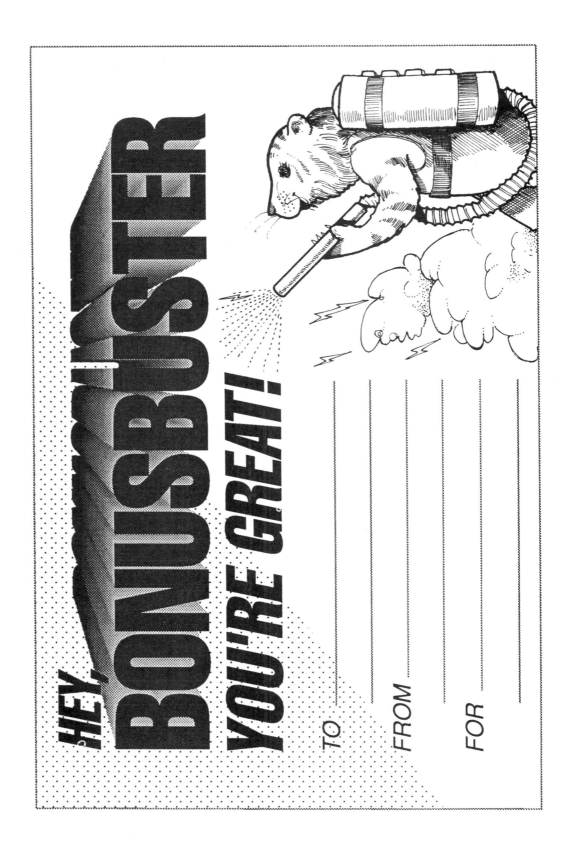

76

GA1172